THE HOW AND WHY WONDER® BOOK OF
The HUMAN BODY

Written by MARTIN KEEN
Illustrated by DARRELL SWEET
Editorial Production: DONALD D. WOLF

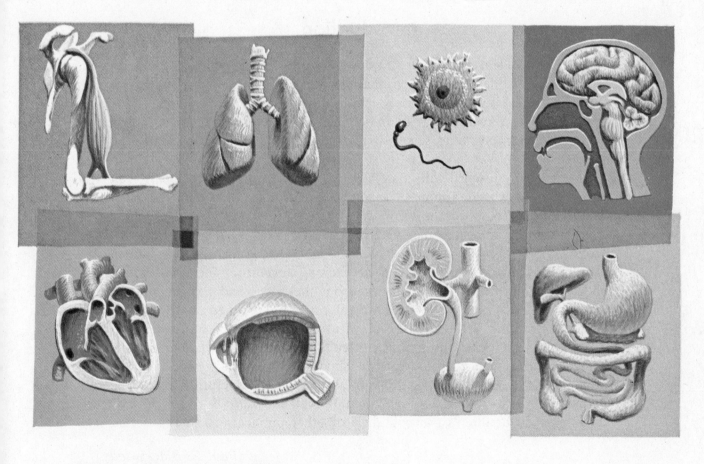

Edited under the supervision of
    Dr. Paul E. Blackwood
    Washington, D.C.

Text and illustrations approved by
    Oakes A. White, Brooklyn Children's Museum, Brooklyn, New York

PRICE/STERN/SLOAN
Publishers, Inc., Los Angeles
1983

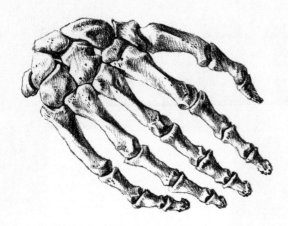

Introduction

It is the habit of scientists to explore, describe and explain all things in the universe. Little wonder, then, that the human body has been a constant object of study, for it is not only important but very close to home! *The How and Why Wonder®Book of the Human Body* tells in a systematic way the most important things scientists and physicians have learned about the subject.

If you simply listened with a stethoscope to the beating of the heart, you might think it was an automatic machine. But if you could tune in on the remarkable activities of the brain cells, you would know that the human body is more than a machine. And as you learn how all the systems work together, you become amazed at what a marvelous organism the human body is. This makes the study of it an exciting adventure, and even though much has been known for centuries about the body, and though more is being discovered every year, there are still many unanswered questions.

The health and well-being of each of us depends on how well we understand our own bodies. This book is written to help us gain that understanding and may encourage many persons to choose a career of service in maintaining the health of others, perhaps as a nurse or doctor. Parents and schools will want to add *The How and Why Wonder®Book of the Human Body* to their children's growing shelf of other publications in this series.

Paul E. Blackwood

Dr. Blackwood is a professional employee in the U. S. Office of Education. This book was edited by him in his private capacity and no official support or endorsement by the Office of Education is intended or should be inferred.

Contents

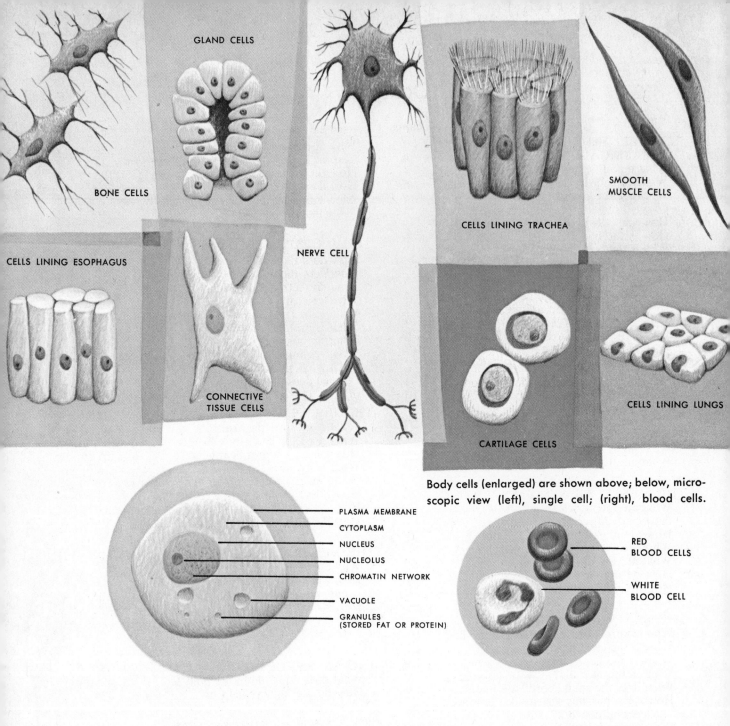

GLAND CELLS

BONE CELLS

CELLS LINING ESOPHAGUS

NERVE CELL

CONNECTIVE TISSUE CELLS

CELLS LINING TRACHEA

SMOOTH MUSCLE CELLS

CARTILAGE CELLS

CELLS LINING LUNGS

Body cells (enlarged) are shown above; below, microscopic view (left), single cell; (right), blood cells.

PLASMA MEMBRANE
CYTOPLASM
NUCLEUS
NUCLEOLUS
CHROMATIN NETWORK
VACUOLE
GRANULES (STORED FAT OR PROTEIN)

RED BLOOD CELLS
WHITE BLOOD CELL

The Cell, the Body's Building Material

What do all living things have in common?

Perhaps at some time you have visited a zoo. There you saw huge elephants, tall giraffes, comical little monkeys, strange birds and many other kinds of animals. The animals in the different cages were so different that you must surely believe that they can have little in common.

Yet, all living things actually do have something in common. All living things are made of tiny units, called *cells*. The huge elephant is made of hundreds of billions of cells, and there are little animals whose whole body is but a single cell. The human body, too, is made of cells — billions of them.

Most cells are so small that you need

What do cells look like?

a powerful magnifying lens to see one. Some cells are so small that you could put 250 thousand of them on the period at the end of this sentence. Others, however, are large enough to be seen with the unaided eye. Among these large cells are the roothairs of plants, certain seaweeds, and the eggs of animals.

Cells are of many shapes. Some are round. Others look like bricks with rounded corners. Still others are long and hairlike. Some cells are shaped like plates, cylinders, ribbons or spiral rods.

Looking through a microscope at a

What are the parts of a cell?

single cell from a human body, you can see that the cell is surrounded by membrane. This is the *cell membrane.* It surrounds the cell in the same way that a balloon surrounds the air within itself.

Within the cell membrane is a material that has a grainy appearance. This material is *cytoplasm,* which flows about within the cell membrane. Cytoplasm distributes nourishment within the cell and gets rid of the cell's waste products.

Within the cytoplasm is a large dot. This dot is really a sphere and is the cell's *nucleus.* The nucleus is the most important part of the cell. It directs

the cell's living activities. The way in which the cell uses nourishment and oxygen, the way the cytoplasm gets rid of wastes, the way the cell reproduces — all these functions are regulated by the nucleus. If the nucleus is removed, the cell dies.

The cell membrane, the cytoplasm,

Of what material are cells made?

and the nucleus of all cells are made of a material called *protoplasm.* Protoplasm is a living material and makes a living cell "alive." Scientists have analyzed protoplasm into the elements of which it is made. They have found protoplasm to

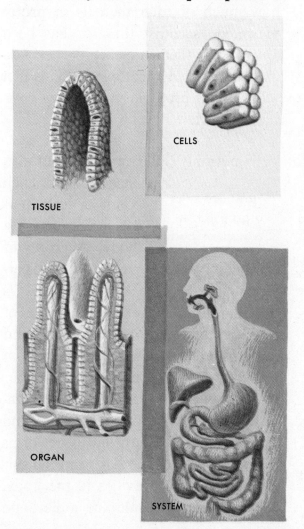

CELLS

TISSUE

ORGAN

SYSTEM

Tiny units are cells; a group of cells is a tissue; tissues form an organ; organs become unified system.

The amoeba is a microscopic mass of protoplasm. It is shown surrounding an organism on which it feeds.

be made of water and many other chemical substances. Although scientists know what these substances are and how much of each there is in protoplasm, no scientist thus far has been able to put them together properly so as to make living protoplasm. This fact tells us that protoplasm is a very complex material.

Cells not only differ in shape, but also in the work each kind of cell performs within a body. A group of cells, all of the same kind, that performs a particular kind of work, is called a *tissue*. For example, groups of cells that transmit impulses back and forth from the brain to other parts of the body make up nerve tissue. Other kinds of tissue are muscle tissue, connecting tissue, supporting tissue, and epithelial tissue. Epithelial tissue forms the outer layer of the skin, and the surface layer of the cavities in the body, such as the nose, throat, gullet and the stomach.

How are cells organized in a human body?

When different kinds of tissue are organized to perform a particular kind of work within a body, the tissues form an *organ*. An eye is an organ that performs the function of seeing. There are many parts to an eye and each part is made of a particular kind of tissue. When all the tissues of the eye work together while each tissue performs its separate task, then the eye can perform its function of seeing. Other examples of organs are the heart, liver, tongue and lungs.

Organs of the body are organized into unified *systems*. Each system performs a particular task for the body. For example, the digestive system, which includes the mouth, teeth, tongue, gullet, stomach, intestines and many glands, performs the function of digesting food.

How is the body like a machine?

Perhaps you have heard an automobile repairman say that a car's ignition system needed fixing. Or maybe it was the cooling system or the brake system. Each one of these systems is made up of several parts, and each system performs a particular task in running the car. All systems must work together if the car is to operate. Do you see the similarity between the automobile's systems and the organ systems of a human body?

The human body is a very wonderful machine. It is more complex, better made and can do more kinds of work under more conditions than any machine that man has so far constructed throughout his history.

Man has built giant electronic calculators that can solve mathematical problems in a fraction of the time that a human brain can. Calculating, however, is the only work the giant machine can do. It cannot decide what problems it should work on, nor when it should work on them, as the slower but more versatile human brain can. The great calculating machine, with its limited capacity, takes up all the space around the walls of a large room, but the human brain, with its unlimited capacity, can easily fit into a shoe box.

Why is the body more useful than a machine?

The calculating machine has thousands of parts, but the number of its parts does not even begin to equal the hundreds of millions of unit cells of which the human body is constructed. If the calculating machine breaks down, it must wait for a repairman to fix it. A break or a cut in some part of the human body can usually be repaired by the body itself.

Let us see in detail how this wonderful machine, the human body, works.

The Skin

When you look at a human body, the first thing you see is the *skin*. The average adult human body is covered with about eighteen square feet of skin. The skin varies in thickness. It is very thin over the eyelids, and quite thick on the palms of the hands and the soles of the feet.

How much skin is on a human body?

The skin is composed of two layers. The upper layer is the *epidermis*. This layer is made of dead, flattened cells, which are continually wearing off as we move around.

What are the parts of the skin?

This is a cutaway view of a single hair (right) showing the follicle, which is the opening, or depression, from which the hair grows.

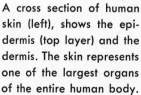

A cross section of human skin (left), shows the epidermis (top layer) and the dermis. The skin represents one of the largest organs of the entire human body.

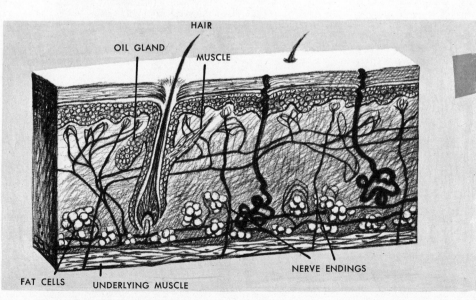

OIL GLAND • HAIR • MUSCLE • NERVE ENDINGS • FAT CELLS • UNDERLYING MUSCLE

The bottom of the epidermis is made of live cells that die and replace those that wear off on the surface.

Beneath the epidermis is the *dermis*. This layer of skin is made entirely of living cells. There are many small blood vessels and nerve endings in the dermis. Small coiled tubes in this layer open into the epidermis. These tubes are *sweat glands* and their openings are called *pores*. Hairs grow out of the skin and have their roots in the dermis. The openings from which hairs grow are called *hair follicles*.

The skin provides the body with a covering that is airtight, waterproof and, when unbroken, a bar to harmful bacteria.

What does the skin do?

The pigment, or coloring matter, of the skin screens out certain harmful rays of the sun.

The skin helps to regulate the temperature of the body. When the body surface is cold, the blood vessels in the skin contract and force blood deeper into the body. This prevents the body from losing much heat by radiation. When the body is too warm, the same blood vessels expand and bring more blood to the surface of the skin. This allows the body to lose heat by radiation. Also, the sweat glands pour out perspiration. The perspiration evaporates, and since evaporation is a cooling process, the skin is further cooled.

When perspiration flows out of the

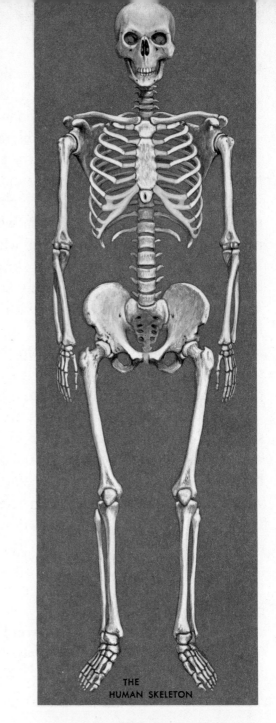

THE
HUMAN SKELETON

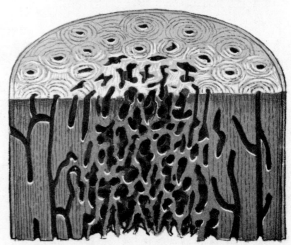

Cross section of human bone. Adults have 206 bones.

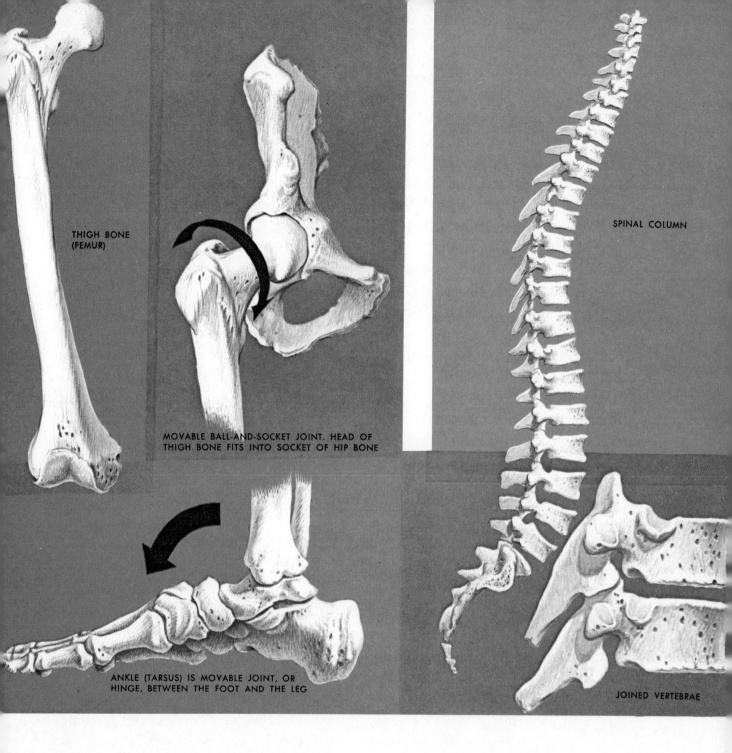

THIGH BONE
(FEMUR)

MOVABLE BALL-AND-SOCKET JOINT. HEAD OF
THIGH BONE FITS INTO SOCKET OF HIP BONE

ANKLE (TARSUS) IS MOVABLE JOINT, OR
HINGE, BETWEEN THE FOOT AND THE LEG

SPINAL COLUMN

JOINED VERTEBRAE

pores, it carries with it certain dissolved body wastes.

The skin is a sense organ because there are many nerve endings in the skin.

Although people do not ordinarily consider the skin to be an organ of the body, you can see by its structure and all the things it performs for the body that it really is an organ.

The Bones

What is the purpose of the skeleton?

If you suddenly removed the poles from a circus tent, the tent would collapse. The poles support the soft, pliable canvas of the tent. They also help to give the tent its shape. The *bones* of the human skeleton support the softer parts of the body

9

and give the body its general shape. If the skeleton of a body were suddenly removed, the body would sink to the floor in a shapeless mass.

The bones also help to protect the softer parts of the body. The skull forms a strong case for the very soft brain. Two bony sockets in front of the skull protect the eyes. The spinal column forms a bony tube that protects the delicate spinal cord. The ribs form a hard elastic framework that protects the heart and lungs. If a person had no ribs and bumped into someone, even a small bump might collapse the lungs or damage the heart.

Bones also provide anchors to which muscles are attached, and bones provide leverage for the movement of the muscles.

There are two other things that bones do for the body: the inner parts of some bones make blood cells; and bones are the body's chief storage place for calcium, a chemical element very important to the sound health of the body.

You can see, by looking at a cutaway view of a bone, that

What is the structure of a bone?

it consists of two main kinds of material: a dense outer material and a spongy, porous inner material. The hard outer material, that gives a bone its shape and strength, is made mostly of compounds of the chemical elements *calcium* and *phosphorus*. The soft inner part of the bone is called *marrow*. Most marrow is yellowish in color. It is made up of fat cells and is simply a storage depot for fat. Toward the ends of long bones, like those of the arms and legs, and generally throughout the interior of flat bones, such as those of the skull and the spinal column, there are patches and streaks of reddish tissue. This reddish tissue gets its color from red blood cells.

Long bones are generally cylindrical in shape. The long, cylindrical portion of these bones is called the *shaft*. The ends of the long bones are thicker than the shaft, and are shaped so that they may fit into the ends of adjoining bones. The short bones, such as those of the wrist and ankle, are composed mostly of a thick shaft of elastic, spongy material inside a thin covering of hard bone material. Flat bones, such as the ribs, are made up of spongy material between two plates of hard bone.

An infant may have as many as 350 bones, but as the

How many bones are there in the human body?

child grows older, many of these bones grow together to form single bones. A normal adult has 206 bones. Some adults may have a bone or two more, because the bones they had as infants did not grow together correctly. Some adults have a bone or two less, because the growing-together process went too far, and two bones of their ankles or wrists that should have remained separate may have grown together.

The skull is made up of twenty-nine bones. The round part of the skull, the part that encases the brain, is called the *cranium,* and consists of eight bones. The face, including the lower jaw, consists of fourteen bones. There are three tiny bones in each ear. And

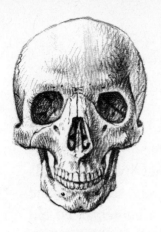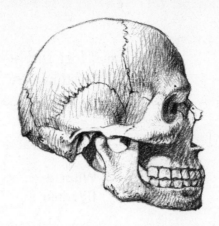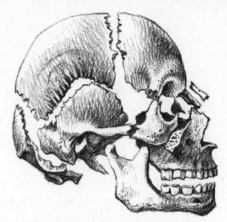

Front view of the human skull (left); side view (center); and side view with bones separated (right). The cranium, the part of the skull enclosing the brain, is composed of bones which are held together by immovable joints.

there is a single bone — the *hyoid bone* — in the throat.

The spinal column consists of twenty-six hollow cylinders of bone called *vertebrae*. If you strung together twenty-six spools of thread on a stiff wire in the shape of a very open letter S, you would have constructed something that looks much like the human spinal column.

The chest consists of twenty-five bones: one breast bone, called the *sternum,* and twenty-four ribs. Seven pairs of ribs attach to the spinal column at one end and the sternum at the other. Three pairs of ribs attach only to the spinal column, curve around to the front, but do not meet the sternum. And two pairs of ribs, called *floating ribs,* extend from the spine only part-way around to the front.

There are two collar bones, and two shoulder bones. Each arm consists of one upper-arm bone and two lower-arm bones. There are eight bones in the wrist. The palm of each hand is made up of five bones, and fourteen bones make up the fingers of a hand.

There are two hip bones. Each leg has one thigh bone, one kneecap, one shinbone, and one bone on the other side of the lower leg.

The ankle of each foot consists of seven bones and the foot, itself, of five, while fourteen bones make up the toes of each foot.

Every bone in the body — except one — meets with another **How are the bones connected?** bone. The one bone that does not meet another bone is the U-shaped hyoid bone in the throat.

The meeting places of the bones are called *joints*. There are two kinds of joints: those about which the adjoining bones do not move, and those about which the bones do move freely. The bones of the cranium are held together by joints of the first kind. These are immovable joints.

Holding these bones together is a kind of very tough, springy **What holds the bones together?** tissue, called *cartilage*. Cartilage also joins together the bones of the spinal column. The springy nature of cartilage makes it a good shock absorber. If the lower parts of the spine receive a blow, the cartilage rings that join each vertebra to the one above it, absorb the shock, so that the brain does not feel the blow. If this were not so, every time you took a step, your brain would receive a jolt.

The bones at movable joints are held together by thick cords of tough, stringy tissue called *ligaments*. To aid movement, at least one of the two adjoining bones has a small hollow that contains a lubricating fluid. This fluid helps the bones move smoothly over one another, just as oil helps the parts of an engine move over one another.

What are ligaments?

All the bones of the body and their connecting cartilage and ligaments make up the body's *skeletal system*.

The Muscular System

The bones of the human body have no way of moving themselves. The muscles of the body move the bones and there are more than 600 muscles to move the parts of the skeleton. Muscles make up more than half the weight of the human body.

What are the muscles?

Muscles are made of bunches of

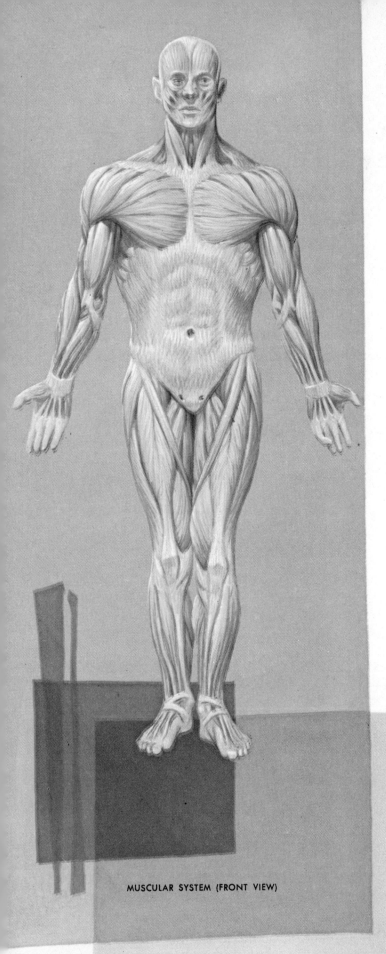

MUSCULAR SYSTEM (FRONT VIEW)

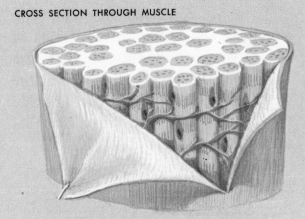

CROSS SECTION THROUGH MUSCLE

muscular tissue held tightly together. Muscular tissue is very fibrous, so that a muscle is somewhat like a bunch of rubber bands bound tightly together.

Beef is the muscle of steers. With a pin,

How can you see muscle fibers? pick apart a piece of roast beef. You will easily be able to separate it into long, thin strands that are fibers of muscle tissue. If you have a microscope, place a very thin muscle fiber under a cover-glass upon a glass slide. You will then be able to see that muscle tissue is made up of spindle-shaped cells.

A typical muscle is thick in the middle

How are muscles attached to bones? and tapers gradually toward the ends. It is the ends of a muscle that are attached to bones. One end of a muscle is anchored to a bone that the muscle cannot move. This attachment is called the *origin* of the muscle. The other end is attached to a bone that the muscle is intended to move. This attachment is called the *insertion* of the muscle. For example, the

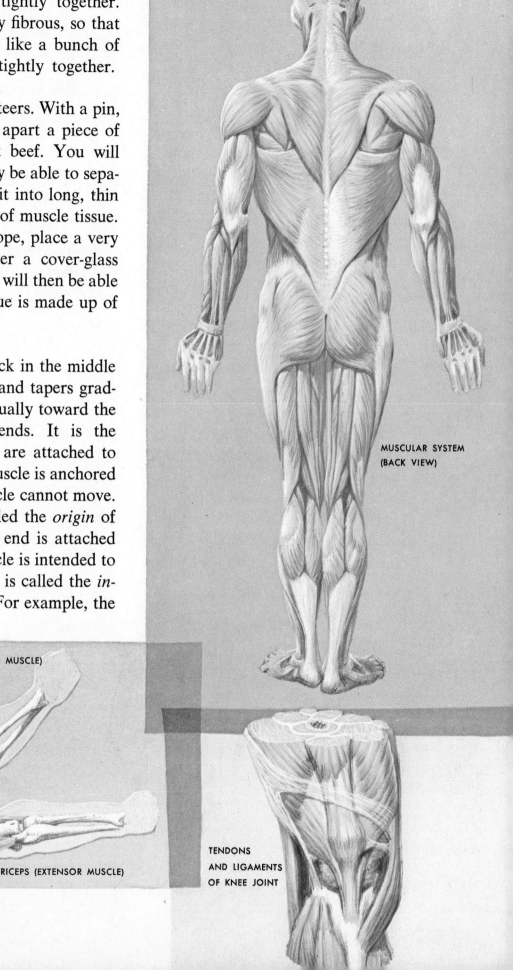

MUSCULAR SYSTEM
(BACK VIEW)

BICEPS (FLEXOR MUSCLE)

TRICEPS (EXTENSOR MUSCLE)

TENDONS
AND LIGAMENTS
OF KNEE JOINT

muscle at the front of the upper arm — called the *biceps* — has its origin at the shoulder bone, and its insertion is just below the elbow joint on the bone that is on the thumb side of the forearm. The actual attachment of the end of a muscle to a bone is usually accomplished by a short, tough cord of much the same kind of tissue that makes up ligaments. This connective cord is called a *tendon*.

All the muscles of the body and their tendons make up the *muscular system* of the body.

The muscles that move the skeleton are ones that we can move at will. They are called *voluntary muscles*. Among them are the ones that move the eyes, tongue, soft palate and the upper part of the gullet.

What are the two kinds of muscle?

There are muscles in the body that we cannot move at will. These are called *involuntary muscles*. This type of muscle is found in the walls of veins and arteries, stomach, intestines, gall bladder, the lower parts of the gullet and in several other internal organs. Thousands of tiny involuntary muscles in the skin move the hair. When you are chilled or frightened and have goose flesh, or goose pimples, the little lumps on your skin are due to the tiny muscles in the skin pulling your hairs erect.

The eye provides a good distinction between voluntary and involuntary muscles. Voluntary muscles enable you to control the movements of your eye, in order to look in the direction you wish. However, you cannot control at will the muscle that widens and narrows the pupil of your eye. This muscle is involuntary.

What are the differences in muscles?

But the distinction between voluntary and involuntary muscles does not always hold true. For instance, when you shiver with cold or fright, the muscles that shake your body are voluntary muscles. Ordinarily, you can control these muscles, but , when shivering, you have no control over either starting or stopping the action of these muscles.

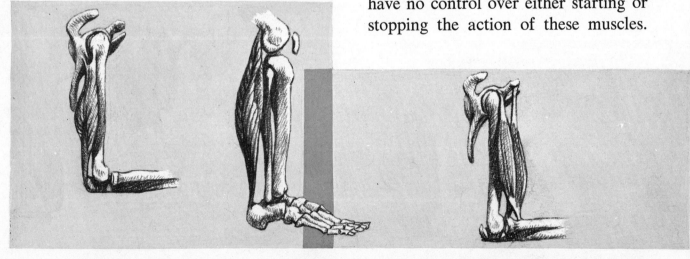

Lowering the arm (left) is an example of a first-class lever, as in a seesaw; rising on the toes (center), a second-class lever, as in a rowing oar; flexing, or "making a muscle" (right), a third-class lever, as in a fishing rod.

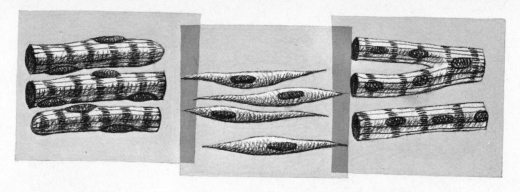

They act as if they were involuntary. Certain circus performers can swallow various objects, and then, at will, bring them up without difficulty. These performers have learned to control their involuntary stomach and lower-gullet muscles, as though they were voluntary muscles.

How do muscles move? Muscle tissue is made of cells whose cytoplasm can contract. When the muscle contracts, it becomes short, and thereby pulls on the bone in which it is inserted. When you want to show someone how strong you are and you "make a muscle" by contracting your biceps, your forearm is pulled up toward your shoulder. If you want to lower your arm, you relax your biceps and contract your *triceps,* the muscle on the underside of the arm. The contraction of the triceps pulls the forearm straight. You can see that the two muscles of the upper arm work as a team or pair. All the voluntary muscles of the body work in pairs.

How do joints help muscles to move bones? One way to increase the power used to do work is to apply that power to a lever. A lever is a device that increases work power or range of motion. The joints in the human body act as levers that increase the power of a muscle or increase the distance through which the muscle can move a bone.

If you raise yourself on your toes, you are making use of one kind of lever. The muscles that form the calves of your legs have to do the work of lifting your whole body. You would need to have much larger calf muscles if they had to undergo the strain of lifting your body by a direct pull. Yet you easily raise yourself on your toes, because your foot acts as a lever.

In the act of raising yourself on your toes, your weight bears straight down on the point where your shinbone rests on your ankle bone. The muscles of your calf pull upward on your heel bone, and your foot pivots upward on the fulcrum — the point around which the lever moves — which is formed by the bones that make up the ball of your foot. (Although we say that we raise ourselves on our toes, we actually raise ourselves on the balls of our feet and steady ourselves with our toes.)

If you reach down and grasp the back of your foot just above your heel, you can feel the strong tendon — called the *Achilles tendon*—that connects the muscles of your calf to your heel bone. If, now, you raise yourself on the ball of your foot, you can feel the calf muscles tighten and bulge as they contract and pull upward on your heel.

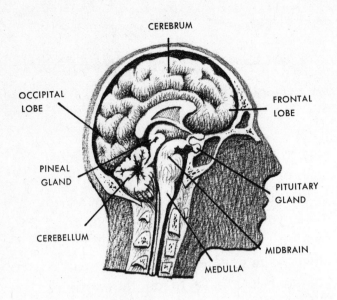

Cutaway view of the skull showing location of brain.

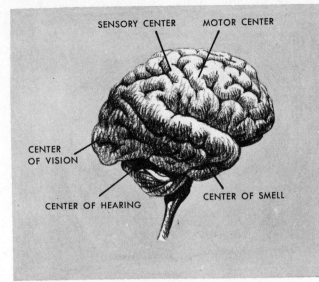

Parts of the brain control several of our activities.

The Brain and Nerves

Suppose you have dropped your pencil on the floor and want to pick it up.

What controls the movements of the body?

This is a very easy thing to do, something you can accomplish with hardly any thought or difficulty. Yet this simple action causes you to use dozens of your voluntary muscles.

First, you have to locate the pencil. This requires you to move your eyes, and probably also to turn your head, until you have brought the pencil into view. Then you must bend down to reach the pencil, grasp it, and then straighten up again. Not only do dozens of voluntary muscles bring about your motions, but they must do so in just the right order. It would be futile to attempt to grasp the pencil before you bent down to bring your hand within reach. Clearly something is controlling the motions of your muscles. What is it?

The movements of your muscles are controlled by your brain which works through a system of nerves distributed throughout your body. The brain and the nerves, together, make up the body's *nervous system.*

The brain occupies the upper half of the skull. The largest part of the brain, called the *cerebrum,* consists of two deeply-wrinkled hemispheres of nerve tissue, one hemisphere on each side of the head.

What is the cerebrum?

All of man's conscious activities are controlled by his cerebrum. It enables him to remember, perceive things, solve problems and understand meanings — in short, to think. Thanks to man's most highly-developed cerebrum, he is the most intelligent of all animals.

At the back of the skull, and almost covered by the cerebrum, is the *cerebellum.* This part of the brain, too, consists of two hemispheres.

What is the cerebellum?

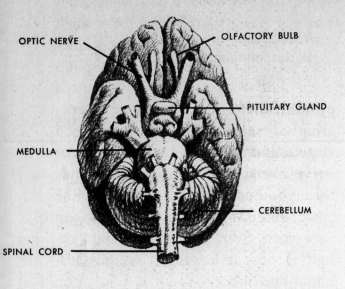

OPTIC NERVE

OLFACTORY BULB

PITUITARY GLAND

MEDULLA

CEREBELLUM

SPINAL CORD

An undersurface view of the brain showing its parts.

The brain and spinal cord make up the central nervous system. The nerves which branch out of this nervous system form the peripheral nervous system.

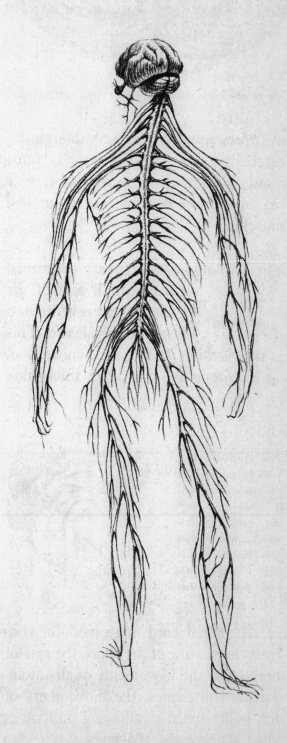

The cerebellum coordinates muscular activity. It is the cerebellum that is responsible for man's ability to learn habits and develop skills. As an infant you learned, after many tries and falls, to stand upright. Learning to walk was another accomplishment that took much time and effort. Now, standing and walking are habits to which you need give no thought, yet both these activities require the use of many muscles in exactly the right order. The cerebellum automatically controls these muscles.

Have you learned to skate or ride a bicycle? At first, you had to think about each move you made, but soon the movements became automatic, so that you did not have to think unless an unusual situation arose. When you were learning, your cerebrum was in control of your movements as you thought about just which muscles you were going to use next. Later, when you knew how to make each movement correctly, your cerebellum took over con-

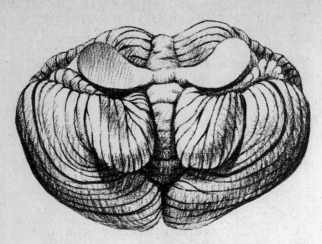

The cerebellum coordinates man's mind and muscles.

trol from your cerebrum. Although the cerebellum's muscular control is automatic, it is important to remember that the muscles it controls are voluntary muscles.

The involuntary muscles are controlled

What is the medulla?

by a small part of the brain that is at the top of the spinal cord. This is the *medulla*. It is a little more than an inch long and is really a thickening

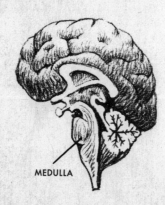

The medulla is a bulblike enlargement of the spinal cord. It carries and sends out nerve impulses which control circulation of blood, breathing, digestion and other processes, too.

MEDULLA

of the spinal cord. The medulla controls the beating of the heart, the rate of breathing, the movements of the stomach and intestines, the movements of the gullet when swallowing and other vital activities of the body.

The *spinal cord* extends downward from

What does the spinal cord look like?

the medulla through the protecting bony rings of the spinal column. The cord is cylindrical in shape, with an outer covering of supporting cells and blood vessels, and an inner, H-shaped core of nerve fibers. The spinal cord extends through four-fifths the length of the spine, and is a little longer in men than in women, averaging sixteen and one-half inches in length. It weighs just about one ounce.

Twelve pairs of nerves branch off the spinal cord and pass through the base of the skull into the brain. Thirty-one other pairs branch off the spinal cord throughout its length. These nerve branches run to all the organs of the body, where they branch again and again, until the smallest branches are nerves which are so thin that they cannot be seen with the unaided eye.

Nerves that extend upward from the spinal cord to the brain pass through the medulla where they cross. Thus, the left side of the brain controls the right side of the body, while the right side of the brain controls the left side of the body.

An army division is composed of many

How is the nervous system like an army telephone network?

thousands of men who perform a wide variety of duties. In order

to control the activities of so many soldiers, it is necessary to have some system by which the commanding general can learn what is going on in all the units of his division and thus, to give orders to any of these units. In order to accomplish this, a telephone network is set up.

When a battle is in progress, soldiers posted near the battle line can telephone reports of action back to their headquarters in order to inform the general of the situation. The general gets the messages from these posts. Using this information, and calling on his training and experience, he issues orders to be followed by soldiers under his command. These orders travel back along the same telephone wires.

Let us follow a similar situation within the human body. Let us suppose that you have accidently knocked a pencil off your desk and want to pick it up. When the sound of the falling pencil reaches your ears, it causes elec-

trical impulses to move from your ears along two nerves — auditory nerves — and then to your brain. Your ears are similar to the posts near the battle line, your nerves similar to the telephone wires, and the electrical impulses similar to the messages that move along the wires.

When the brain receives electrical impulses from the ears, a particular part of the cerebrum perceives the impulses as sound, and passes this information on to another part of the cerebrum, one that is concerned with recognition. This part of the brain calls on the part that stores information —

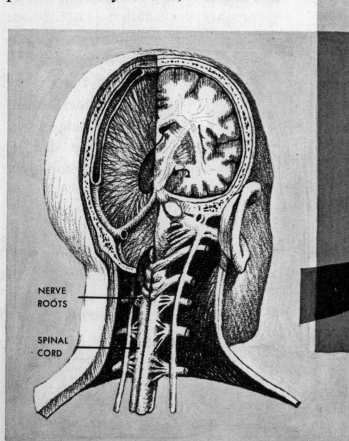

NERVE ROOTS

SPINAL CORD

(Left): Cutaway view of back of the head. (Above): Part of the backbone, also known as the spine, spinal column and vertebral column. It consists of bones called vertebrae which surround the spinal cord.

19

the memory. If you have ever before heard a pencil fall, your memory recognizes the sound. Now, you are aware of what has happened.

This situation is similar to that of the general who gets battle reports, and then calls on his training and past experience to help him get a clear picture of what is taking place at the battle-front.

Once your brain is aware of the fallen pencil, it decides to pick up the pencil. Electrical impulses go from your brain to the muscles of your eyes, which then move about seeking to bring the pencil into view. This is similar to that of the general who sends messages to front-line posts asking for more information on the battle.

When the pencil is brought into view, electrical impulses flash back to your cerebrum, which must again go through the processes of perception and recognition, in order to identify the pencil. Here we have new reports coming back to the commanding general who interprets them.

Having located the pencil, your cerebrum now sends hundreds of electrical impulses along nerves to the many muscles that must be moved when you bend over, reach out your arm, close your fingers around the pencil, and then straighten up again. These impulses and the responding muscular movements are similar to messages from the general going out over the telephone wires and the soldiers acting upon the general's orders.

Nerve cells, also called *neurons,* are specially constructed **What are nerve cells?** so as to carry nerve impulses from one part of the body to another. Nerve tissue can conduct extremely small amounts of electricity. Nerve impulses are actually small amounts of electricity.

Each neuron has a central portion, or *cell body,* that has a **What are the parts of a neuron?** nucleus, cytoplasm and a cell membrane. From one side of the cell body there extend very slender branching threads of protoplasm.

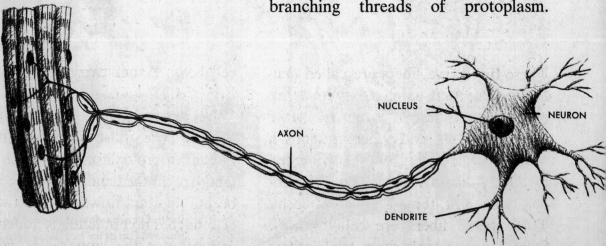

NUCLEUS

AXON

NEURON

DENDRITE

Nerve impulses from a neuron travel to the nerve endings of a muscle (left).

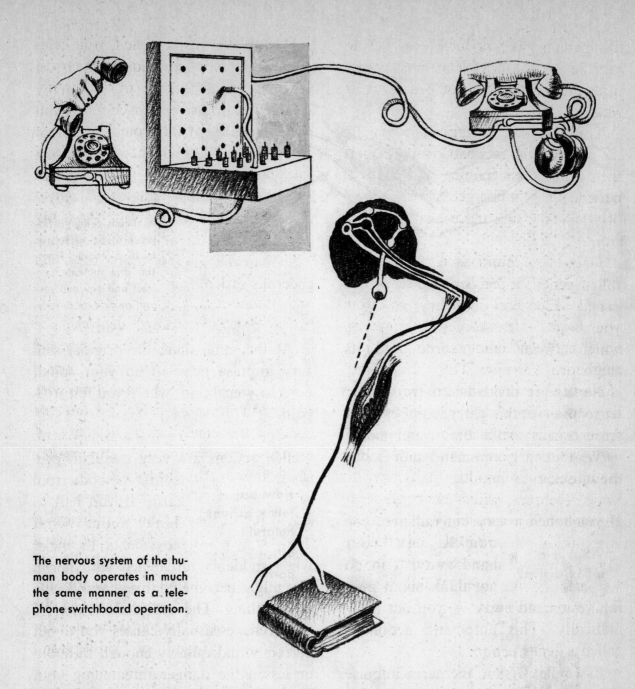

The nervous system of the human body operates in much the same manner as a telephone switchboard operation.

These tiny nerve fibers are called *dendrites*. They look much like twigs at the end of a tree branch. From the other side of the cell body there extends a fairly thick nerve fiber — surrounded by a fatty sheath — which ends in slender, branching threads of protoplasm. These nerve fibers are called *axons*. Some axons are very short, while others are as much as three feet long. Dendrites conduct nerve impulses to the cell body. Axons carry impulses away from the cell body.

Nerve tissue is made up of a series of neurons arranged so that the branching threads of protoplasm of an axon intermingle with the dendrites of the neighboring neuron. However, the two sets of branches do not actually touch. The gap between the branches is called a *synapse*. When an impulse moves along a nerve, it must jump across the syn-

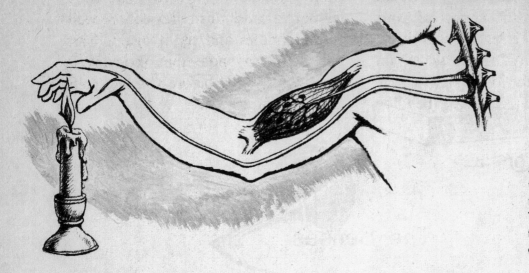

A simple reflex action takes place when you touch a candle flame. The arm muscles contract and you pull your arm away very quickly.

apse between one neuron and its neighbor.

Nerves are divided into two kinds: *sensory nerves* that carry impulses from sense organs to the brain, and *motor nerves* that carry command impulses to the muscles.

If you touch a very hot radiator, you

What is a reflex action?

quickly jerk your hand away. You do not think about pulling your hand away — you act automatically. This automatic action is called a *reflex action*.

In a reflex action, the nerve impulse takes a special pathway, called a *reflex arc*. In the case of your touching the hot radiator, the impulse moved from the skin where it came in contact with the radiator along a sensory nerve to your spinal cord. Here the impulse set off another impulse in a motor nerve running from your spinal cord to your arm muscles. The muscles contracted and pulled your hand away from the radiator. This action took place in about one-tenth of a second.

At the same time, the original sensory impulse traveled up your spinal cord to your brain, where you felt it as pain.

Reflex actions are very useful in pro-

How are reflex actions helpful?

tecting the body from harm. If you had to think about what movements to make when suddenly threatened with harm, you might become confused and do the wrong thing. The automatic action of your reflexes usually causes you to act correctly and quickly enough to avoid or lessen the danger threatening you. For example, if you suddenly become aware of an object flying through the air toward your face, reflex actions cause you to dodge the object and to close your eyes tightly.

Sit comfortably in a chair, and cross

How can you demonstrate a reflex action?

your right leg over the upper part of your left leg. Feel around just below the

kneecap of your right leg for a tendon

that runs downward from the kneecap. With the edge of the fingers of your right hand strike this tendon sharply — though not too hard, of course. If you do this correctly, the lower part of your right leg will jump upward, bending from the knee joint. After you have learned to cause this reflex action, wait a few minutes and try it again. This time, you may note that your leg is already in motion before you feel your fingers strike the knee.

The Senses

We are made aware of the world around us by means of our *senses*. For many centuries, man believed that human beings had only five senses: *sight, hearing, touch, smell,* and *taste.* Modern scientists have added to the list the senses of *pressure, heat, cold* and *pain.*

What are the senses?

There are several steps in the process of sensing. A stimulus acts on the nerves in one of the sense organs. Nerve impulses from the sense organ travel to the brain. In the brain, the impulses are interpreted as a feeling or sensation. For instance, if you stick your finger with a needle, nerve endings in the skin of your finger are stimulated to send impulses to your brain, which interprets the impulses as pain.

It is important to note that, although the brain interprets the impulses as pain, the pain is not felt in the brain, but rather in the finger; that is, the sense organ.

The organs of sight are the *eyes.* A human eye is shaped like a ball and is about an inch in diameter. The eye is surrounded by a tough white protective covering. At the front of the eye, there is a transparent circular portion in this covering. Just behind this transparent portion is a space filled with a clear liquid. At the back of this space is a circular tissue with a hole in it. The tissue is called the *iris,* and the hole is the *pupil.* The iris is the colored part of the eye. On the

What does the eye look like?

CROSS SECTION OF THE HUMAN EYE

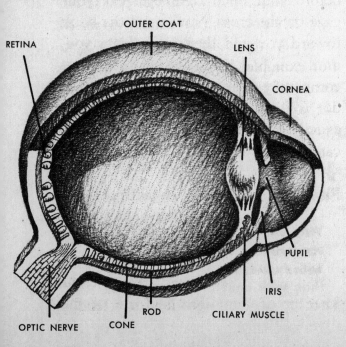

RETINA
OUTER COAT
LENS
CORNEA
PUPIL
IRIS
CILIARY MUSCLE
ROD
CONE
OPTIC NERVE

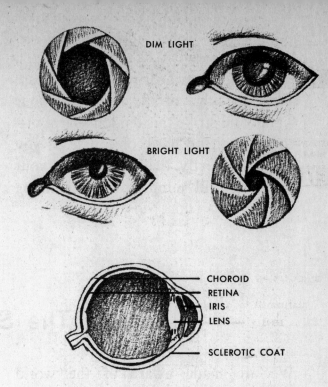

DIM LIGHT

BRIGHT LIGHT

CHOROID
RETINA
IRIS
LENS

SCLEROTIC COAT

inner edge of the iris, around the pupil, is a ring of tiny muscles sensitive to light. In bright light, these muscles contract and narrow the pupil. In dim light, the muscles relax and widen the pupil.

If you stand in front of a mirror in a brightly-lit room, you can easily see the pupil of your eye widen and narrow. Cover one eye with your hand for about a minute and a half. Suddenly remove your hand, and look at the eye that was covered. You will see the pupil narrow.

How do we see? Behind the iris is a transparent circular lens made of tough tissue. Muscles attached to the rim of this lens can focus it upon near or far objects. A beam of light passing through the lens is turned upside down and is reversed from right to left. After passing through the lens, light traverses a large spherical cavity that makes up the bulk of the eye. This cavity is filled with a clear liquid through which light passes easily. Around the inner surface of this cavity is a coating of special nerve endings that are sensitive to light. This sensitive coating is the *retina*. The nerve endings connect with the *optic nerve* that leads to the brain.

Light, reflected from an object and entering the eye, is focused by the lens as a reversed image on the retina. The nerve impulses arriving at the brain from the retina are interpreted as an image of the object.

This interpretation also reverses the directions of the image as it was projected on the retina, so that we do not see things upside down and backward.

What is the blind spot? At the point where the optic nerve enters the eye, there is no retina, and consequently, this area is not light-sensitive. This point, which is just below the center of the back of the eye, is called the *blind spot*.

You can prove the existence of this blind spot in the following manner. Note the cross and the dot on this page. Close your left eye, and hold this page before your open right eye. Fix your gaze on the cross. Now move the book toward you and then away from you, until you find the point where the dot completely disappears. At this point the dot is focused by the lens of the eye exactly on your blind spot. Hence, you can't see the dot.

✚   ●

Why do we see better with two eyes than with one? Place a table directly beneath a light, so that objects near the center of the table cast no shadows. Stand about eight feet in front of the

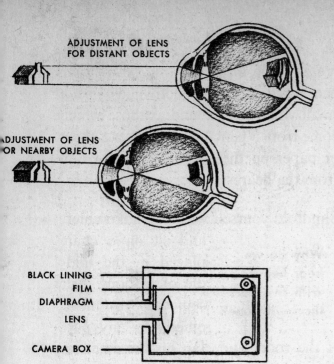

ADJUSTMENT OF LENS
FOR DISTANT OBJECTS

ADJUSTMENT OF LENS
FOR NEARBY OBJECTS

BLACK LINING
FILM
DIAPHRAGM
LENS

CAMERA BOX

table. Crouch down so that your eyes are on a level with the top of the table, and close one eye.

Ask someone to stand a thread-spool at the center of the table. Also ask him to place another spool of the same size about four inches in front or in back of the first spool, but not to tell you whether the second spool is before or behind the first. Try to guess the location of the second spool. Try this several times, keeping a record of your correct guesses. You will probably have a poor score.

With both eyes open, repeat your guessing. This time, you should have a nearly-perfect score. Why?

When we look at an object with both eyes, a slightly different image is projected on the retina of each eye. This is true because each eye sees the object from a slightly different angle. The result is that the brain's interpretation of the two images provides the viewer with a single, three-dimensional image of the object. The two images also pro-

vide the viewer with a perception of depth that enables him to make judgments of farness and nearness. This is why you had a better score when judging the locations of the spools with both eyes open.

The *ears* are the organs of hearing. The

What does the ear look like?

part of the ear on the outside of the head helps to a slight extent to direct sound waves into the ear. Sound waves entering the ear strike the eardrum, or *tympanic membrane*, and cause it to vibrate. This membrane stretches taughtly across the whole diameter of the ear passage. Touching the inner surface of the eardrum is a tiny bone called the *malleus* or hammer. The malleus connects by a joint to another little bone, the *incus* or anvil. And the incus is jointed to a third bone, the *stapes* or stirrup — so named because it looks like a stirrup. Below

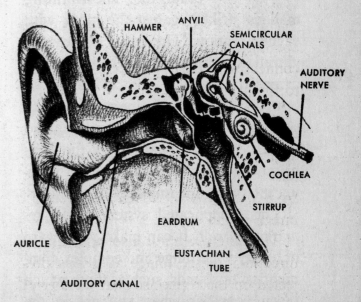

HAMMER ANVIL SEMICIRCULAR CANALS AUDITORY NERVE COCHLEA STIRRUP EARDRUM AURICLE EUSTACHIAN TUBE AUDITORY CANAL

A cross section of the human ear, showing its parts.

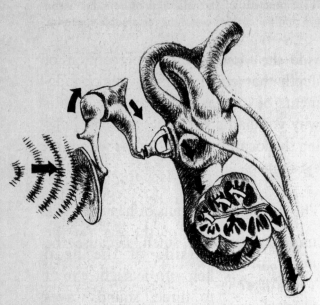

Arrows show path of sound through the inner ear.

and inward from the stirrup are three small cavities filled with liquid that are separated from each other by membranes. The innermost of these membranes connects with nerves that go to the brain.

When sound waves cause the eardrum **How do we hear?** to vibrate, the eardrum causes the malleus to vibrate, too. The vibrating malleus strikes against the incus with each vibration. The incus passes the vibration to the stirrup, which, in turn, causes the liquid in the cavities to vibrate. Vibration in the innermost cavity sets up impulses in the nerves that go to the cerebrum. That part of the cerebrum concerned with the sense of hearing interprets the impulses as sound.

This complicated system works remarkably well. It can make you aware of a very wide range and complex combination of sounds, such as those which reach your ear when you are in the presence of an orchestra. Also, your hearing organs can be activated by such small volumes of sound as those which come from a pencil moving over a sheet of paper on the other side of a room from the hearer.

Blindfold yourself with a handkerchief, **Why do we hear better with two ears than with one?** and sit on a chair placed in the middle of a room. Ask someone to move quietly to any part of the room and clap his hands once. Point to where you think he is. Repeat this activity several times as your aide moves quietly from place to place about the room. Have your helper keep score of the number of times you have pointed correctly to the location at which he clapped his hands.

Place a hand tightly over one ear, and repeat the whole experiment. Repeat it a third time, covering the other ear.

If your sense of hearing is normal, you will find that your score of correct locations was poorer when you listened with only one ear. From this you can readily understand that using two ears gives you a better perception of sound direction, just as using two eyes gives you a better perception of visual depth.

The organ of smell is the *nose*. When **Why do we smell odors?** taking a breath, you may draw into your nose certain gases intermingled with the gases of which air is made. When the added gases come into contact with a small patch of epithelial cells on the upper part of the inner surface of your nose, the cells cause impulses to travel along a pair of nerves to your cerebrum, where the impulses are interpreted as odors.

Just how this process takes place is not clearly known. However, since the inside of the nose is always damp, scientists believe that the odorous gases dissolve in the dampness and cause a chemical reaction that stimulates nerve endings in the epithelial cells. This causes the cells to send impulses along the nerves.

Not all gases react with the organ of smell to set up sensations of odor. This is why we call only certain gases — those that do react — odors or smells. The more of an odorous gas that comes into contact with the organ of smell, the stronger is the sensation of odor. This is why we usually draw deep breaths when we sniff about to locate the source of an odor.

The sense of smell seems to become fatigued easily; **Can the sense of smell get "tired" or "lost"?** that is, the sensation of odor fades after a short time. Perhaps you have entered a room in which you found a strong odor. After a few minutes, however, you did not seem to notice the odor at all.

The discharge of mucus that accompanies a severe cold will cause you to lose your sense of smell, because the mucus forms a thick covering over the epithelial cells of the nose and prevents odorous gases from coming in contact with the cells.

The sense of smell is highly developed among a large part of the animal kingdom. These animals use smell as their chief means of learning about their surroundings. In human beings, however, the sense of smell is only mildly developed.

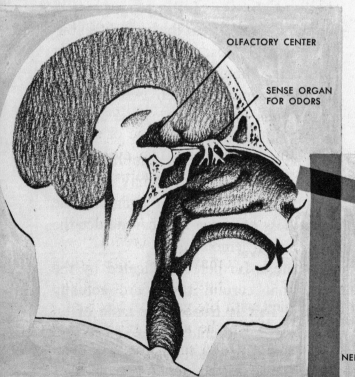

OLFACTORY CENTER

SENSE ORGAN FOR ODORS

The cutaway view of the head shows the sense organ for odors and the olfactory center. The cross section is an enlarged part of the lining of the nose.

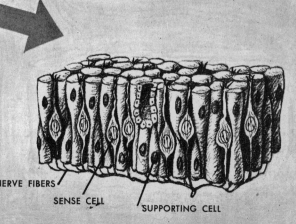

NERVE FIBERS

SENSE CELL

SUPPORTING CELL

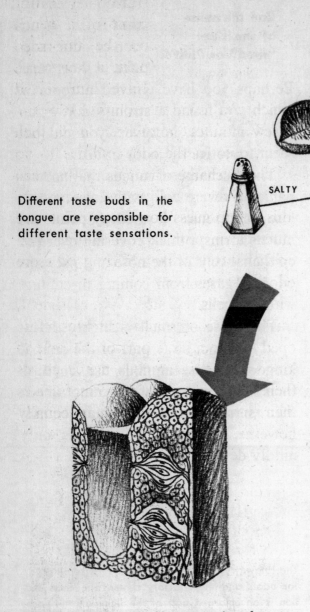

Different taste buds in the tongue are responsible for different taste sensations.

SOUR

SALTY

BITTER

SWEET

Taste buds are shown in this cross section of tongue.

How do we taste things? Small organs, called *taste buds,* are located just below the surface of the tongue and in three places in the throat. Certain materials taken into the mouth cause taste buds to produce the sensation of taste. Just how this sensation is brought about is not known. Taste, like smell, is probably the result of a mild chemical reaction. Taste sensations may be divided into *sweet, salty, sour* and *bitter*.

Not all tastes are detected by the same taste buds. Those taste buds at the sides and tip of the tongue transmit impulses of saltiness to the brain. The buds at the tip of the tongue detect sweetness, those near the base detect bitterness and those on the sides detect sourness. Thus, there are certain areas of the tongue in which two kinds of taste buds are located: these are the sides and the tip.

The sense of taste is complicated by the fact that one taste may mask or counteract another. For example, the sweetness of sugar will counteract the sourness of lemon juice.

Taste is further complicated by the fact that certain tastes are actually odors. This is true of the taste of an onion. If a bad cold causes you to lose your sense of smell, you will not be able to taste an onion.

How do we feel things? The chief organs of feeling are free nerve endings in the epithelial cells of the body. On the outside of the body, the skin is the organ of feeling; within the body, it is the epithelial cells that line all cavities, such as the mouth, throat, stomach, intestines, ears, chest and sinuses.

Not all feelings are detected by the same nerve endings. In the skin there are 16,000 that detect heat and cold and more than four million that detect pain. Still others cause the sensation of touch. This latter sensation is in some way heightened by the hairs of the body. If a hairy portion of the body is shaved, its sensitivity to touch is temporarily reduced.

Sensations of feeling within the body are difficult to explain. Gas that distends the intestine during an attack of indigestion may cause intense pain. Yet surgeons have found that they can cut, burn, pinch and mash the internal organs of a person without causing the patient any pain.

Are all areas of the skin equally sensitive to the touch? Blindfold yourself. Ask someone to press lightly the blunt point of a pencil on the upturned palm of your hand. Have him repeat this action, using the points of two pencils held about a quarter of an inch apart. Let your helper continue to do this, alternating irregularly between one and two pencil points. As he does this, try to guess how many points are pressing on your hand each time. You will probably make a fairly good score of correct guesses.

But if you repeated this experiment, using the skin of your upper back, close to your spine, you would not be able to tell whether one or two pencil points were being used. This demonstrates that not all areas of the skin are equally sensitive to touch.

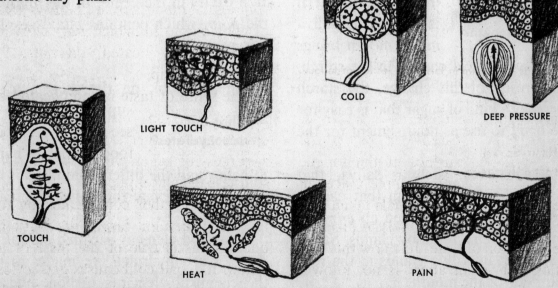

TOUCH

LIGHT TOUCH

COLD

DEEP PRESSURE

HEAT

PAIN

The skin is the organ of feeling. The cross sections show the nerve endings responsible for various sensations.

The Digestive System

How does the body use food?

We have learned that the blood carries nourishment to the cells of the tissues. This nourishment comes from the food we eat. Certainly, food in the form in which we put it into our mouths could not be carried by the blood. Before food is in a form that enables it to nourish the tissues, it must be greatly changed. This process of change is called *digestion*.

The mouth, esophagus (or gullet), stomach, small intestine and large intestine form a continuous tube about thirty feet long called the *alimentary canal*. Food passes through the alimentary canal during the process of digestion. The *liver* and the *pancreas*, two large glands, are also important in the digestion of food. The alimentary canal and these two glands make up the body's *digestive system*.

How does digestion begin in the mouth?

One of the constituents of food is starch. When food that contains starch is chewed, the saliva in the mouth brings about a chemical change in the starch. As a result of this change, the starch becomes a kind of sugar that is easy for the body to use as nourishment for the cells.

A substance, such as saliva, that changes food into a form that can be used by the body is called an *enzyme*. Enzymes are secreted by glands. Saliva is secreted by saliva glands in the roof and floor of the mouth.

Only starch can be digested in the mouth. Fats and proteins, the two other main constituents of food, must be digested farther along in the alimentary canal.

How do teeth aid digestion?

Since food, whether digested in the mouth or other part of the alimentary canal, must be swallowed, the food must first be broken up into small pieces. As we chew, our teeth cut and grind food into small pieces that are wetted by saliva, and finally formed by the tongue into lumps that we can easily swallow.

A tooth is a remarkable structure. The part of the tooth above the gum is the *crown;* below the crown, and covered by the gum, is the *neck;* below the neck is the *root* that lies in the socket of the jaw bone. A tooth has an outside covering of enamel, the hardest material in the body. Inside the enamel, and forming the main part of the tooth, is *dentine*. It looks like bone but is harder. In a cavity in the center of the tooth is the *pulp,* which contains blood vessels and nerves.

What are carbohydrates?

When you look on the shelves of a supermarket, you see such a variety of food that it is hard to believe all the different kinds can be divided into a few food elements. But this is true.

One food element is called *carbohydrate*. Carbohydrates are made up of the chemical elements carbon, hydrogen and oxygen. Starches and sugars, bread and macaroni and rock candy, too, are some carbohydrates. The human body uses carbohydrates as a source of energy. If the body has more carbohydrates than it can use, it may change them into fat, which it stores.

Another food element is *fat,* which is

What is fat? a better source of energy than carbohydrate. Butter, margarine, lard and olive oil are a few examples of fat as well as the white irregular streaks in a beefsteak and around the edges of the steak.

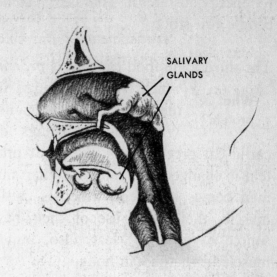

SALIVARY GLANDS

Location of the salivary glands in the human body.

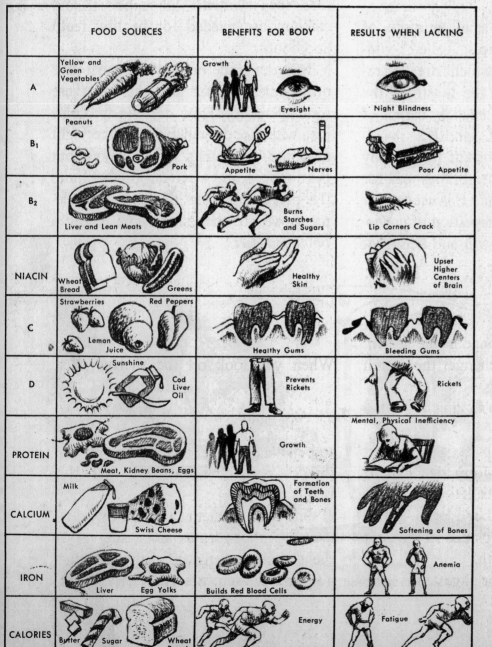

	FOOD SOURCES	BENEFITS FOR BODY	RESULTS WHEN LACKING
A	Yellow and Green Vegetables	Growth — Eyesight	Night Blindness
B₁	Peanuts — Pork	Appetite — Nerves	Poor Appetite
B₂	Liver and Lean Meats	Burns Starches and Sugars	Lip Corners Crack
NIACIN	Wheat Bread — Greens	Healthy Skin	Upset Higher Centers of Brain
C	Strawberries — Red Peppers — Lemon Juice	Healthy Gums	Bleeding Gums
D	Sunshine — Cod Liver Oil	Prevents Rickets	Rickets
PROTEIN	Meat, Kidney Beans, Eggs	Growth	Mental, Physical Inefficiency
CALCIUM	Milk — Swiss Cheese	Formation of Teeth and Bones	Softening of Bones
IRON	Liver — Egg Yolks	Builds Red Blood Cells	Anemia
CALORIES	Butter — Sugar — Wheat Bread	Energy	Fatigue

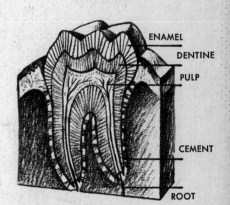

ENAMEL
DENTINE
PULP
CEMENT
ROOT

Cross section of a tooth.

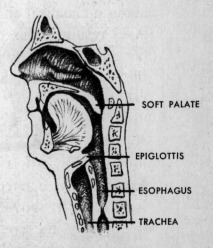

SOFT PALATE
EPIGLOTTIS
ESOPHAGUS
TRACHEA

The process of swallowing.

31

If the body has more fat than it can use for energy, it stores it. That is why some people are stout.

The third main food element is *protein* which is manufactured in the bodies of green plants. When human beings or cattle eat green plants, the plant protein is changed into muscle. When human beings eat meat, which is cattle muscle, they make use of their best source of protein. Meat, also, builds muscle in the human body.

What is protein?

Many foods contain small amounts of substances called *vitamins,* which are necessary to the health of the body. Vitamins are named by means of the letters A, B, C, D, and K.

What are vitamins?

Vitamin A is important for healthy eyes, skin, mucous membranes and for normal growth. Vitamin B is needed for good appetite, good digestion of carbohydrates, normal growth and health of nerves and muscles. Vitamin C is important for growth, the development of teeth, good skin and healing. Vitamin D is needed for strong bones and teeth. Vitamin K is important for the clotting of blood and normal liver function.

Even if we eat enough food, we will not be healthy unless the food contains sufficient vitamins.

Other food elements are called *minerals.* These are small amounts of certain chemical elements. For example, the elements phosphorus and calcium are needed for healthy teeth and bones.

What are minerals?

In order to be healthy, we must give our bodies proper amounts of these food elements. How are we to know just what foods will provide the right amounts? Scientists have worked out the answers, and when our diet includes the proper amounts of each food element, we are then said to be eating a *balanced diet.*

A balanced diet will give the body the nourishment it needs. This is a requirement to maintain good health. A diet that is lacking in certain requirements could lead to a state of unhealth which doctors call *malnutrition.*

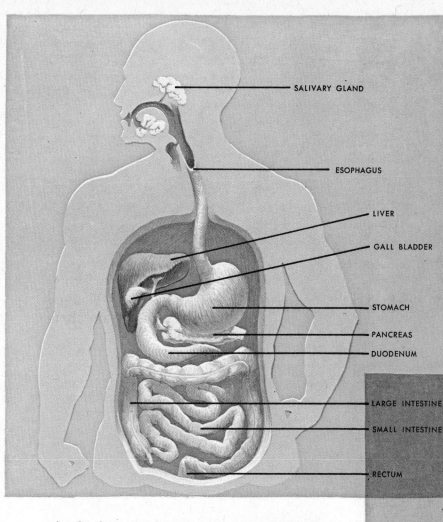

- SALIVARY GLAND
- ESOPHAGUS
- LIVER
- GALL BLADDER
- STOMACH
- PANCREAS
- DUODENUM
- LARGE INTESTINE
- SMALL INTESTINE
- RECTUM

The alimentary canal (including the mouth, esophagus, stomach, small and large intestines), the liver and the pancreas make up the body's digestive system.

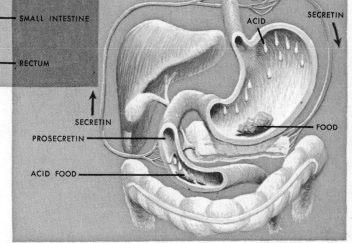

- ACID
- SECRETIN
- SECRETIN
- PROSECRETIN
- FOOD
- ACID FOOD

The stomach and intestine in the digestive process.

Digested food is absorbed through threadlike villi.

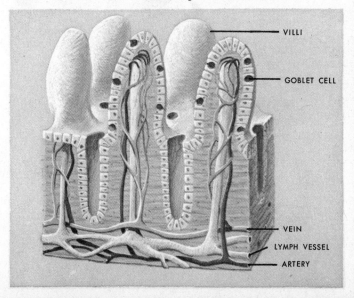

- VILLI
- GOBLET CELL
- VEIN
- LYMPH VESSEL
- ARTERY

A chicken sandwich, for example, contains starch, fat and protein. The bread is mainly starch, the butter is fat and the chicken is protein.

What is the process of digestion?

When a piece of the sandwich is chewed, the starch is being digested by saliva.

When a mouthful of the sandwich is swallowed, it passes into the *esophagus*. This is the muscular tube that contracts along its length to push the food down into the stomach.

In the stomach, which is a muscle, the food is churned about while digestive juices pour in from glands in the stomach wall. Eventually, the churning action moves food out of the stomach and into the small intestine.

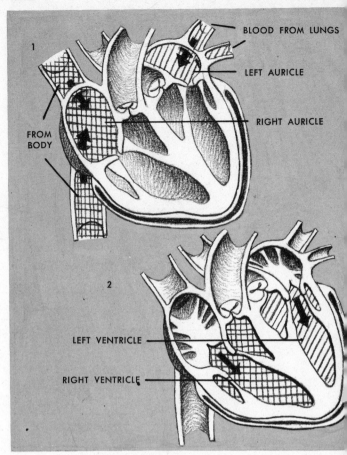

The greater part of the digestive process takes place in the small intestine. Here the protein and the fat are finally changed into forms that can be used by the tissues. The liver contributes to this digestive process by secreting into the small intestine a liquid called *bile*. The pancreas secretes pancreatic juice which further aids in dissolving food.

What does the small intestine do?

The small intestine undergoes continual muscular contraction called *peristalsis*. This action pushes the digested food into the large intestine. The surface of the small intestine has a large number of threadlike projections called *villi*. The digested, liquefied food is absorbed through the villi, and passes into capillaries that are inside the villi. Now, the food is in the bloodstream. As we have learned, the blood carries the food to the cells in the tissues, which use the food to provide the body with energy and material for repair.

Not all the parts of the chicken sandwich can be digested. Those parts which are indigestible pass through the large intestine to its lower part, called the *rectum*. Eventually, the indigestible food is eliminated from the rectum through the *anus*.

The Circulatory System

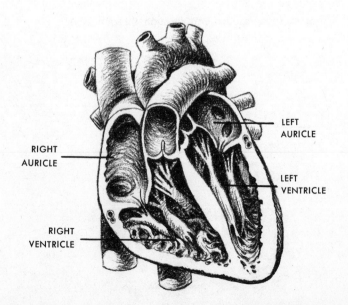

What work does the heart do?

Although the study of anatomy is more than 2,000 years old, it was not until the English physician William Harvey described the circulation of the blood, at the beginning of the 17th century, that men knew what work the *heart* did in the body. The heart had been carefully dissected and described, yet no one knew its use.

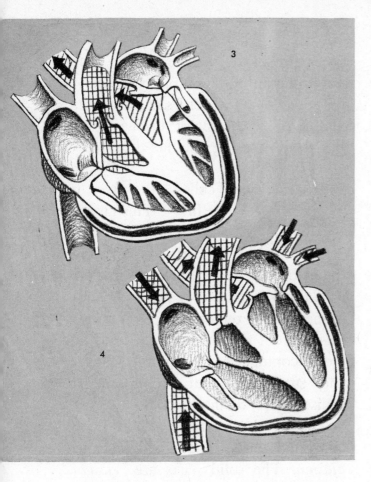

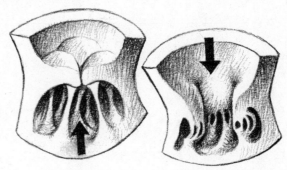

The arrows indicate the direction of blood pressure. Pressure forces closing and opening of the valves.

(1) Auricles contract, squeezing blood into ventricles. (2) Ventricles contract, cuspid valves close, semilunar valves open, blood goes to arteries. (3) Ventricles relax, semilunar valves close, cuspid valves open, blood goes to ventricles. (4) Blood goes to auricles and ventricles, heart relaxes, pauses momentarily.

The heart is a very efficient pump that moves blood through the body. The heart is a muscle that contracts and relaxes about seventy times a minute, for all the minutes of all the years of your life. Each contraction and relaxation of the heart muscle is a *heartbeat*. You have more than 100,000 heartbeats every day. Each heartbeat pumps about two ounces of blood. This results in about 13,000 quarts of blood being pumped each day.

What does the heart look like? The heart is divided into four chambers. The upper two chambers are called *auricles;* the lower two are called *ventricles*. Each auricle is connected with the ventricle below it by a valve that allows blood to flow from the auricle to the ventricle, but not in the opposite direction. The heart also contains a network of nerves that naturally regulates the pumping operation.

One of the wonders of modern surgery is the heart transplant, first demonstrated to be operationally feasible in humans by Dr. Christian Barnard. By this means, the deteriorated heart of a patient who would otherwise not have long to live may be physically replaced by the healthy heart of a person who has just died. Several people have been able to resume normal lives, thanks to this medical miracle.

How can you hear a heartbeat? Obtain two small funnels and a length of rubber tubing about one or two feet long. Into each end of the tube, place the snout of one of the funnels.

Now, place the rim of one funnel on the chest of a friend, and place the other funnel to your ear. The "lub-dupp, lub-dupp, lub-dupp" you hear is the sound of your friend's heart opening and closing. A doctor listens to the heartbeat by using a stethoscope.

Blood has been called "the river of life." This is an appropriate description, because

What work does the blood do?

the blood supplies the cells of the body with the materials they need for nourishment and repair, and it removes wastes from the cells. In addition, the blood contains cells that fight disease and substances that repair cut or bruised parts of the body.

The blood is made up of both liquid and solid parts. The liquid is called *plasma*. The solid parts are *red corpuscles*, *white corpuscles* and *platelets*.

The heart, blood, veins and arteries make up the circulatory system. The aorta carries the blood from the heart, which branch arteries distribute through body.

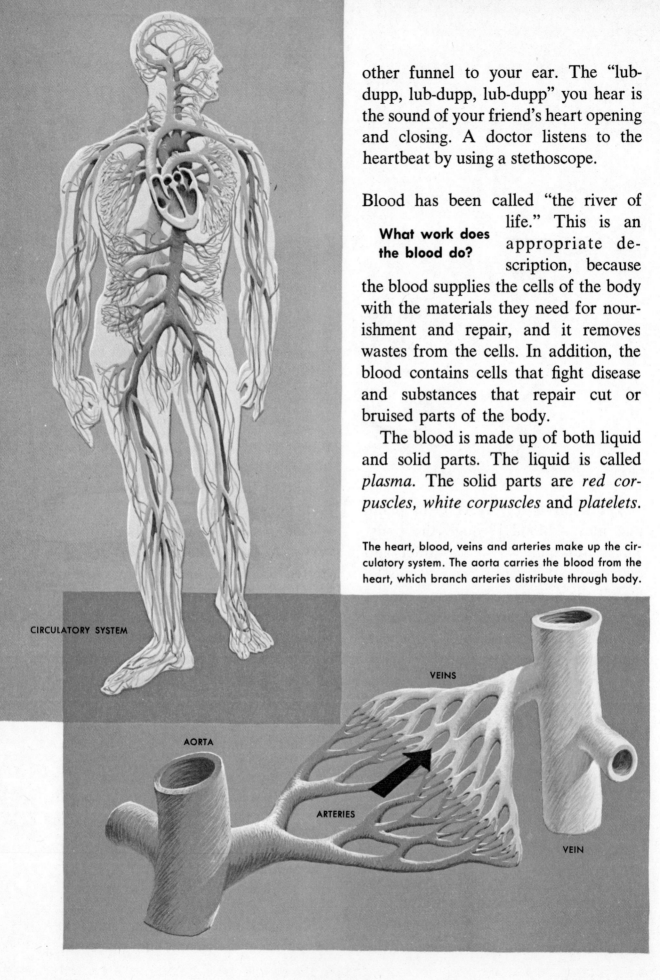

CIRCULATORY SYSTEM

VEINS

AORTA

ARTERIES

VEIN

The word *corpuscle* is the Latin word for "little body."

More than nine-tenths of the blood consists of red corpuscles. They are so small that a large drop of blood contains more than 250 million of them. They are disc-shaped and concave on each side. These corpuscles contain a substance called *hemoglobin*, which is a compound of iron. Hemoglobin can combine very well with oxygen from the air in the lungs. It is the task of the red corpuscles to carry oxygen to cells in all parts of the body, and upon reaching these cells, to give up the oxygen to them.

What are red corpuscles?

When hemoglobin combines with oxygen, it turns bright red. That is why blood running out of a cut is always red — the hemoglobin is combining with the oxygen of the air.

Red corpuscles live only about fifty to seventy days, and thus, they must be replaced continuously. We learned that the interior of a bone contains reddish tissue, which is due to the presence of red blood cells. Within the marrow of some bones, red cells are formed.

If a person lacks sufficient red cor-

Red corpuscles, white corpuscles and platelets make up the solid part of the blood, as opposed to plasma.

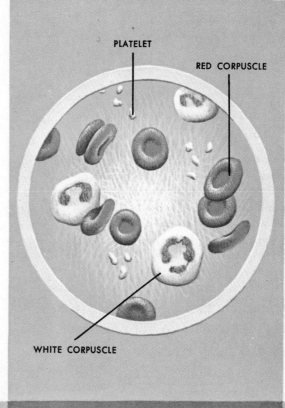

PLATELET

RED CORPUSCLE

WHITE CORPUSCLE

The cross sections, below, demonstrate how the human body uses its own substances to heal surface wounds.

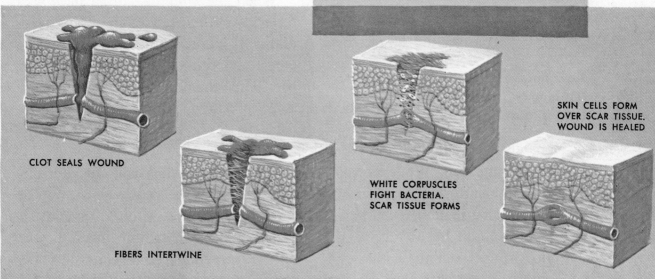

CLOT SEALS WOUND

FIBERS INTERTWINE

WHITE CORPUSCLES FIGHT BACTERIA. SCAR TISSUE FORMS

SKIN CELLS FORM OVER SCAR TISSUE. WOUND IS HEALED

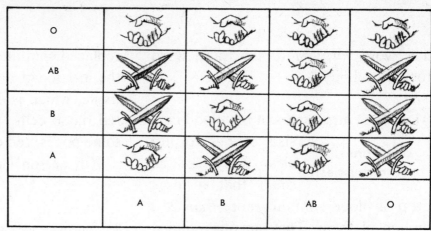

DONOR				
O	🤝	🤝	🤝	🤝
AB	⚔️	⚔️	🤝	⚔️
B	⚔️	🤝	🤝	⚔️
A	🤝	⚔️	🤝	⚔️
	A	B	AB	O

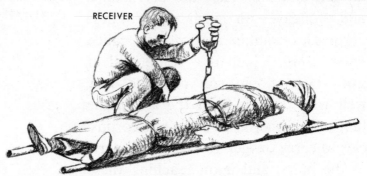

RECEIVER

A Nobel prize-winning scientist, Karl Landsteiner, discovered that there were four main groups of blood in humans, which he classified as A, B, AB and O. This is important because in a blood transfusion, a person with one kind of blood would become ill if he received another kind that did not agree with him. The chart shows which blood types can be given in transfusion to persons with any of the four blood groups. It also shows the type of blood that persons with any of the four blood groups can receive. The symbol of the handshake stands for "agree with." The crossed swords signify "opposed to." All the races have the same four blood types.

puscles, he is said to have the disease *anemia*. He is usually listless and thin, because his cells do not receive enough oxygen. Some types of anemia may be cured by adding sufficient iron to an anemic person's diet.

Most white corpuscles are larger than red ones, and there are fewer white corpuscles in the blood than red ones. For approximately every 800 red cells there is only one white cell. White corpuscles have no definite shape, and move about by changing their shape.

How does the blood fight disease?

Disease is caused by an overabundance of harmful bacteria within the body, and it is the function of the white corpuscles to destroy bacteria. To destroy a bacterium, a white cell moves over to the bacterium and then engulfs it. Once the bacterium is inside the white cell, it is digested.

When large numbers of harmful bacteria invade the blood, the body automatically increases the number of white corpuscles produced by the bone marrow. Then the body has sufficient white cells to destroy most of the invading bacteria.

You know that when you cut yourself, the blood flows out of the wound for only a short time. Then the cut fills with a reddish solid material. This solid is called a *blood clot*. If blood did

How does blood clot?

not clot, anyone with even a slight wound would bleed profusely. Indeed, the blood of certain persons does not clot, a condition known as *hemophilia*.

The platelets are the particles in the blood responsible for causing it to clot. When blood flows from a cut, it carries platelets. When air comes into contact with the platelets, the oxygen in the air causes the platelets to disintegrate and release a substance that combines with certain substances in the plasma. This combination forms a substance called *fibrin*. Fibrin is in the form of a network of tiny threadlike fibers that trap the cells of the blood to form a dam which holds back the further flow of blood.

Since the heart pumps so much blood,

How does blood move through the body?

it must be clear that the same blood must pass through the heart many times in the course of a day. This is true, for the round trip of blood from the heart to distant parts of the body and back takes less than a minute. The round trip to nearer parts of the body takes an even shorter time.

The blood takes two main paths in its trip through the body. When the right ventricle of the heart contracts, blood is forced into a large artery that leads to the lungs. (An *artery* is an elastic tube that carries blood away from the heart.) Here the red cells of the blood take up oxygen from the air in the lungs. They also give up carbon dioxide.

From the lungs, the blood flows through two veins that lead back to the heart. (A *vein* is an elastic tube that carries blood toward the heart.) The blood enters the left auricle and passes through the valve leading to the left ventricle. When the left ventricle contracts, the blood flows into another large artery. This artery branches into smaller arteries that branch several times more into smaller and smaller arteries. The smallest arteries are in the tissues, and are called *capillary* arteries. From the capillaries, the blood transfers nourishment and oxygen to the cells and removes carbon dioxide and other wastes.

Capillary arteries connect with capillary veins. These tiny veins connect with larger and larger veins as they approach nearer to the heart. Blood flowing through the veins eventually reaches a large vein that enters the right auricle of the heart. From the right auricle, the blood flows through the valve leading to the right ventricle, and thus it ends a complete round trip through the body.

The heart, the blood and the veins and arteries make up the body's *circulatory system*.

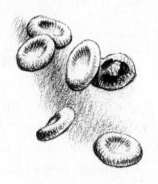

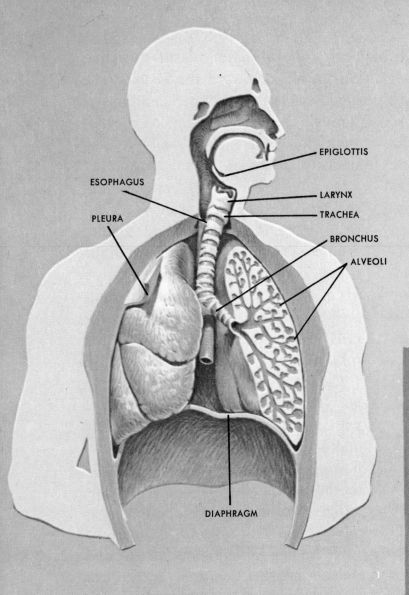

ESOPHAGUS
PLEURA
EPIGLOTTIS
LARYNX
TRACHEA
BRONCHUS
ALVEOLI
DIAPHRAGM

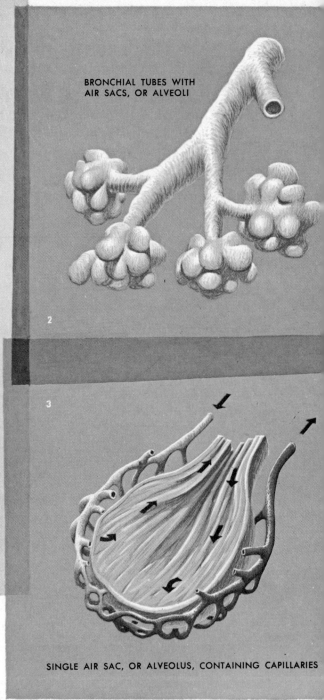

BRONCHIAL TUBES WITH AIR SACS, OR ALVEOLI

SINGLE AIR SAC, OR ALVEOLUS, CONTAINING CAPILLARIES

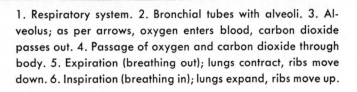

1. Respiratory system. 2. Bronchial tubes with alveoli. 3. Alveolus; as per arrows, oxygen enters blood, carbon dioxide passes out. 4. Passage of oxygen and carbon dioxide through body. 5. Expiration (breathing out); lungs contract, ribs move down. 6. Inspiration (breathing in); lungs expand, ribs move up.

The Respiratory System

Why do we breathe? We have learned that the cells of the body need oxygen, and that the oxygen is obtained from the air. In order to obtain oxygen, we must first get air into our bodies, which we do by inhaling, or breathing in.

Across the body cavity, and below the lungs, is a flat, powerful muscle called the *diaphragm*. When this muscle is moved downward, it causes the ribs to move upward and outward. The result is a partial vacuum that is produced in the lungs. The pressure of the

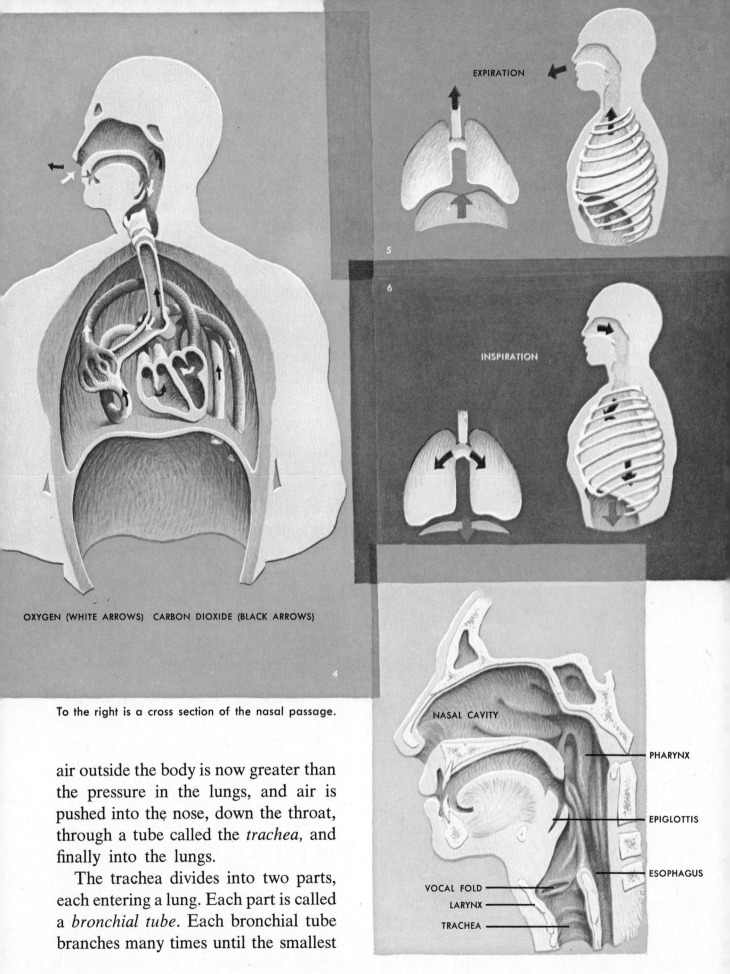

OXYGEN (WHITE ARROWS) CARBON DIOXIDE (BLACK ARROWS)

EXPIRATION

INSPIRATION

NASAL CAVITY

PHARYNX

EPIGLOTTIS

ESOPHAGUS

VOCAL FOLD

LARYNX

TRACHEA

To the right is a cross section of the nasal passage.

air outside the body is now greater than the pressure in the lungs, and air is pushed into the nose, down the throat, through a tube called the *trachea,* and finally into the lungs.

The trachea divides into two parts, each entering a lung. Each part is called a *bronchial tube.* Each bronchial tube branches many times until the smallest branches are almost as small as capillaries. These smallest branches are called *alveoli*. The tissues that make up the alveoli contain capillary arteries and veins.

Oxygen passes from the air through the walls of the arteries, and combines with the red blood cells. Carbon dioxide passes through the walls of the veins, and into the air in the lungs.

When the diaphragm relaxes, the ribs move downward, compress the lungs, and force the carbon-dioxide-rich air out of the lungs by the same path through which it entered.

To do this, you must obtain a bell jar,

How can you make a model breathing apparatus?

a one-hole rubber stopper that will fit the jar, a glass tube in the shape of a Y, two small balloons and a large thin piece of rubber.

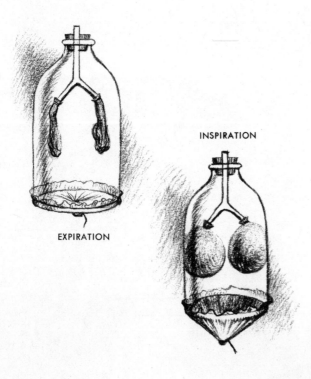

INSPIRATION

EXPIRATION

Place the stopper in the mouth of the jar. Tie the two balloons to the ends of the arms of the Y-tube. Put the other end of the glass tube into the hole in the stopper, doing so by way of the bottom of the bell jar. Tie the large piece of rubber around the bottom of the bell jar.

By pulling downward on the bottom of the large piece of rubber, which represents the diaphragm, you will simulate the breathing process. The upper part of the tube represents the trachea, the arms represent the bronchial tubes, and the balloons represent the lungs.

One way that the cells of the body use

How is air important to the body cells?

the nourishment brought to them by the blood is in providing energy for the body's movements. To provide this energy, certain parts of the nourishment stored in the cells must be combined with oxygen. The oxygen is obtained from the air through the breathing process, and is taken to the cells by the red corpuscles.

When you run you use up more energy.

Why do you breathe more deeply when you run?

This energy must come from the combination of oxygen with the stored nourishment in the cells. The process of combination must take place on a larger scale than usual. To bring this about you need more oxygen in your blood. By breathing more deeply you get more oxygen in your lungs and, thereby, more oxygen in your blood.

The Excretory System

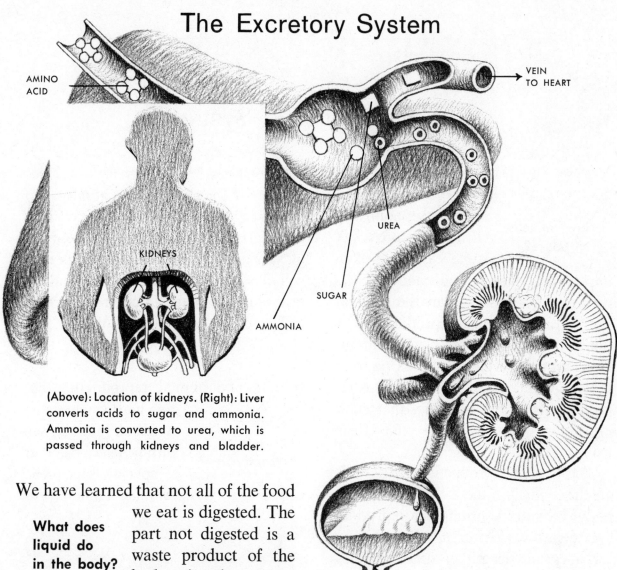

AMINO ACID

VEIN TO HEART

UREA

SUGAR

AMMONIA

KIDNEYS

(Above): Location of kidneys. (Right): Liver converts acids to sugar and ammonia. Ammonia is converted to urea, which is passed through kidneys and bladder.

What does liquid do in the body? We have learned that not all of the food we eat is digested. The part not digested is a waste product of the body. Another waste product about which we have learned is the air which contains carbon dioxide.

We drink many liquids, some of which provide us with nourishment. Milk is such a liquid. The foods we eat are largely water. The water is quite useful, because, upon entering the bloodstream, it keeps the nourishing food materials dissolved so that they can pass through the membranes of the cells of tissues. It also dissolves waste products within the cells. Somehow, the plasma of the blood, which is partly water, must get rid of the dissolved waste products.

How do the kidneys help us? This task is performed by the *kidneys* which are at the lower part of the back, above the hips. Each kidney contains millions of tiny coiled tubes. Blood flows through these tubes and the liquid waste products in the blood are filtered out. These liquid wastes pass from the kidney into a sac where they are temporarily stored. This storage sac is the *bladder*. Every so often, your bladder becomes sufficiently full so as to cause you to want to empty it, a process called *urination*.

ASEXUAL
REPRODUCTION

The Reproductive System

Living things can reproduce themselves, but nonliving things cannot. A stone can be broken into several pieces; and each piece is permanently smaller than the original stone. Living things reproduce other things that closely resemble the parent. Dogs reproduce themselves as puppies that grow into dogs. Human beings reproduce themseves as babies that grow into adult humans much like their parents.

How do cells reproduce?

The unit of reproduction is the unit of the body — the cell. Within the body, cells are continuously reproducing themselves. After a cell has lived for a certain length of time, changes take place within its cytoplasm. These changes soon cause the cell to begin to narrow at the middle. Eventually, the narrowing process pinches the cell into two cells. But the changes in the cytoplasm have made certain that each new cell has all the parts a cell needs in order to live and function. The new cells soon grow to the size of their parent cell. Then the new cells split in two.

Human and animal reproduction begins with single cells. A female animal has within her body, in a special sac, cells called *egg cells.* A male animal pro-

What is the process of reproduction?

duces in his body certain cells called *sperm cells*.

If a sperm cell comes in contact with an egg cell, the sperm cell is absorbed by the egg cell. This absorption causes the egg cell to begin to reproduce itself by splitting in two. This splitting process goes on until the original egg cell has become thousands of cells.

These thousands of cells form a hollow ball. As reproduction of the cells in the ball continues, one side of the ball caves inward, creating a double-walled hemisphere.

Up until now, the cells in the hemisphere have all seemed to be of the same kind. Now, as the reproduction of cells continues, different types of

Human beings produce children by the process of reproduction. When a sperm cell, the male sex cell, joins with an egg, the female sex cell, the egg becomes fertilized. The fertilized egg develops into billions of cells that form an embryo, which is the name given to a baby during its first few months of development in the mother's body. Later, the developing infant is called a fetus. It takes about nine months for a child to be born. This nine-month period is known as pregnancy or the gestation period.

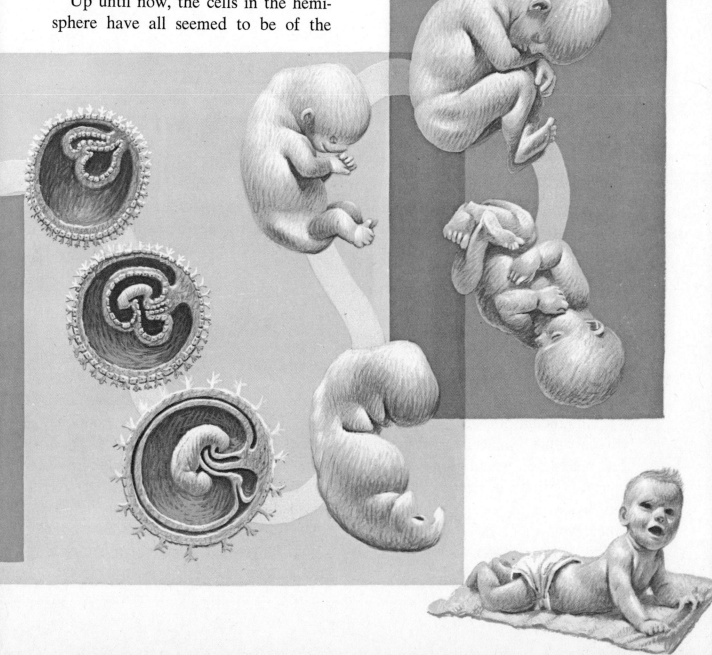

cells form in different parts of the new living thing. In other words, tissues begin to form.

The process of the reproduction of cells in mammals may go on for many months. During this time, what was once a ball of cells begins to form all the parts of the animal's body.

This whole process takes place in the body of the mother animal. The part of her body that holds the newly-forming animal is called the *uterus*. At last, a whole small animal has been formed as the result of continuous cell reproduction. When this time arrives, the muscles of the uterus contract, and the fully-formed little animal is pushed out of the uterus — that is, it is born.

In human beings, the complete process of reproducing a new human being — a baby — takes just a little over nine months.

Your Body and Your Person

We have learned about the parts of the body-machine. When all these parts are put together, we not only have a human body, but also a person.

Why is the human body more than a machine?

What makes us a person is nothing that we can see or touch. It is the fact that we love and want to be loved, have ideas, plan things, daydream, feel sorrow and pity — in short, to do the things that make you human.

Suppose that you and a friend were both hungry, and then you came upon a small amount of food. If you were to act only like a machine satisfying its fuel needs, you would eat all the food yourself. However, since you are a human being, as well as a human machine, you share the food with your friend, even though your fuel needs may not be completely met.

When a machine is fueled, it works until it needs more fuel. The human machine not only does this, but it plans ahead for the time when there will be no more fuel. In other words, human beings know their food will run out, so they plant crops, hunt and fish.

Human beings have *emotions*. It is not easy to say just what an emotion is, but love, hate, sadness, happiness, anger and tenderness are some emotions. All human beings have emotional needs — the need to experience certain emotions. All persons need to be loved, to feel a little bit important, to feel needed and to have new experiences. Attempts to satisfy these needs are the main things that spur human beings to act as they do.

What are emotions?

Care of the Body

Need for exercise: Everyone needs some exercise in order to keep the muscles in good condition. When we remember how much of the body is made up of muscles, we realize the importance of this conditioning. The object of exercise is to cause the heart to pump a little faster. This forces a little more blood into capillaries in the tissues, and makes certain that every part of the body is being nourished and having its waste products removed. It also causes deeper breathing, thereby emptying out carbon dioxide from sacs in the lungs that are ordinarily not used.

The right amount of exercise gives a feeling of well-being, not fatigue.

Need for rest: Very strenuous exercise or exercising for too long may produce fatigue. Fatigue is caused by wastes accumulating in the body. When muscles are moving continuously or are under strain, they produce more waste products than the body can immediately rid itself of. When this happens, the body needs rest, in order to catch up on waste removal. Sleep is the best kind of rest and one should get enough sleep every day.

Care of the skin: There are many skin diseases, some of which are caused by germs. Others are due to substances to which the skin is very sensitive. For example, boils are caused by an infection of certain bacteria commonly found on the

". . . All work and no play makes Jack a dull boy . . ."

skin. Fungus growths can also cause skin diseases. Dirty, neglected skin can result in infestation by insects, such as lice.

A clean skin will either completely eliminate the possibility of these skin ailments, or will lessen the presence of the things that cause them, to the point where the natural protective functions of the body can handle such threats.

The skin should be thoroughly washed with mild soap at least once a day. If an infection or a fungus growth does take place, a physician should be consulted.

Care of the eyes: The eyes are probably the most valuable sense organs. They should not be exposed to very bright sunlight. In the presence of bright sunlight, sunglasses give adequate protection.

One should always have sufficient

light when reading or writing. Rest the eyes occasionally by looking into the distance or by closing them once in a while.

Never rub the eyes with dirty towels or hands. An infection may result.

The eyes should be tested regularly — at least once a year, or more frequently as the case may be — by an eye doctor.

Above all, never try to treat any eye trouble yourself. Always obtain the help of a physician.

Those who have healthy skin will probably also have healthy hair and nails. Hair can be kept clean only by washing, and a thorough shampoo once a week is usually sufficient. But if the hair is particularly oily, it may have to be washed more often. Brushing the hair frequently stimulates the circulation in the scalp, and also helps to remove dirt, loose hairs and dandruff.

Care of the hair and nails:

Most dandruff is not a disease. The outer layer of the skin naturally flakes off, and these flakes may cause mild dandruff. However, if the scalp is also very oily and reddened, it may indicate the kind of dandruff that requires the help of a physician.

If the nails dry and split easily, proper food elements in the diet may be lacking. A balanced diet frequently clears up this condition.

Never poke any hard object into the ear — it may break the eardrum. Glands in the ear secrete a substance called ear wax. The purpose of this secretion is to keep the eardrum pliable. Sometimes these glands secrete too much wax, which blocks up the ear canal and impairs the hearing. If this happens, do not try to remove the wax yourself. Get the help of a doctor.

Care of the ears:

Keep the ears clean by washing them with soap and water, and use nothing sharper than a finger to wash in the opening of the ear canal.

Particles of food left in the mouth after a meal provide nourishment for bacteria. Bacteria secrete a substance which can dissolve the enamel of the teeth, and thereby cause cavities. For this reason, the teeth should be brushed after each meal whenever possible. This will remove the food particles, and prevent the action of the bacteria.

Care of the teeth:

Since it is not always possible to prevent all decay, even by regular brushing of the teeth, a dentist should be consulted two or three times a year.

The hygienic care of the body becomes especially meaningful when we remember that good health is largely dependent on a body which functions properly. Good health to you all!